and THE MAPLE *will turn* GREEN AGAIN

MONA CHATTA VIJAY

ISBN 979-8-88606-688-3

With gratitude and reverence

to

K.L. Chatta & Nalini Chatta,

(Dad and Mom)

Vijay, my husband, for always being there to encourage me,

And my children Akshay and Kritika in motivating me to embark on this journey…….

Contents

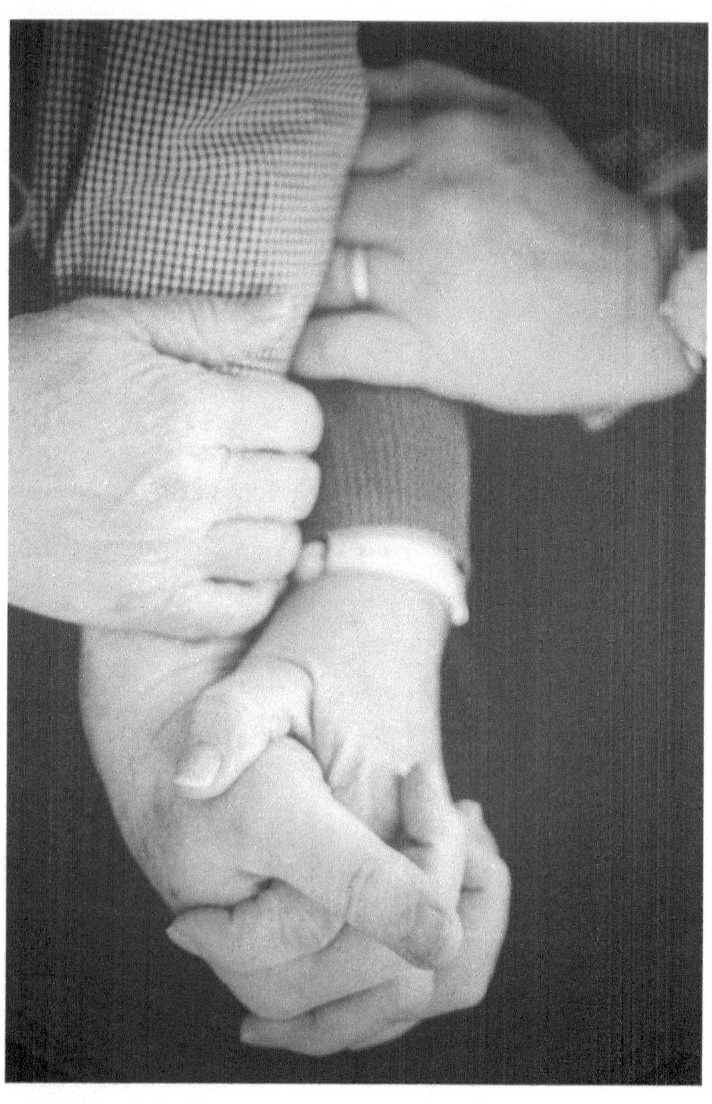

From Grandparents' Heart

We are now old and we just want a smile, love and respect;

We want you to love us, be with us.

We have lived our life and devoted ourselves to our family,

Now, it's your turn to reciprocate.

We don't want expensive gifts;

All we need is love, respect and empathy.

We want you to understand we exist;

We too are significant,

We too are affectionate,

We weren't always like this, old and broken;

We too were once like you – vigorous and agile.

The growing years have not been easy,

With age, we need rest, we need love.

We need you to understand us,

Together, with your parents, we can give you a sound foundation,

You will remember after we are gone.

For us you will always remain,

Our love, our pride.

But yeah, we need you to be with us,

To understand us and make us feel we too are important,

We celebrated your arrival and we always will.

We just need some patience, some understanding,

We are not wicked, we are not useless,

We are like an old tree with very firm branches,

You can always rely on.

Let's always be for each other,

And enjoy this togetherness, learning from each other,

And understanding each other.

(I clicked this picture of the Rangeet river in January 2020, just a few months before Covid 19 engulfed the globe. We had gone to Sikkim to ring in the New Year and this river provided me with the serenity that I required).

The Journey

I started off early, very much in time,

Knowing fully that this beautiful world was mine,

Saw the stars and the moon on my way, shine;

Things so attractive that I forgot time.

This delay on the way, I knew, would take its toll,

And keep me away from reaching my goal,

The flowers and the breeze had changed their colours,

And I now knew that the world was theirs.

I was shattered, things were pell- mell;

I realised people that I trusted had stabbed me on my back,

Why does it always happen this way?

The people you trust the most,
Always turn you away.

A bubbly, carefree and a friendly soul,
Had been turned into a ghoul!
Who is to be blamed?
Is it you or me?

Before pointing fingers at someone,
Remember, you are causing him pain.
Conditions never remain same for anyone,
Today it's me, tomorrow it could be you.

(The teacher in me always finds it interesting to read my students' faces and expressions. I scribbled the following poem while invigilating one of the exams. The poem is very close to my heart. I feel their faces reflect their parents' dreams.)

Thinking of My Students

For us they will always remain,
Tiny souls seeking advice.
No doubt they're growing,
And drifting away from us, yet,
They'll always remain a part of us.

When chided, occasional frowns do occur,
They exhale few curses too,
Without getting hurt we should,
Move ahead on our path.

It's all a part of growing up,
Growing saplings need their space,
Or they perish!

These fledglings have become stronger,
They have faith in their wings,
Let's not alter their faith and
With guidance show them the way.

Say It When You Must

Where is the time to hate?
How do we get time to hate?
When life is so short lived……
When each moment is so uncertain.

Celebrate each moment as it comes,
Live each moment as it unfurls,
Celebrate each little joy as it comes,
For no one has seen tomorrow!
Cherish each moment.

Don't stop your thoughts from flowing,
Don't choke your emotions,
Say something when you want to say it,
Don't wait for tomorrow,
For no one has seen tomorrow.

Each moment is so uncertain,

Life may not give another chance, so,

Say it when you must.

The Dilemma

It's a struggle to keep going,

When people you trust, turn your tormentors.

When the wind blows against you,

And you struggle to stay stable.

When eyes are full …

but you create dams to check the flow,

when the heart bursts with pain,

but you manage a smile.

When your world has crashed, but

you show everything is fine,

when you are tired, unable to move,

but forced to move that extra mile.

When you want the end to be near,

But it just doesn't come.

When your emotions have dried up,

But you have to smile.

When you are concerned for people,

Who just don't care.

When you know that everything is a farce,

And you still keep up with it.

When you want to smile,

but your lips are sealed.

When you want to see the colours,

but the eyes don't oblige.

When you want to sing lovely songs,

but your chords have run dry.

When you want to enjoy the world,

but your brain goes numb.

It's a struggle to keep going….

Why can't you just break the shackles…..

And be free!

For ever, for ever…….

To All with Love

What do you do when the trust is gone?
Cry over what's happened or await dawn?
Wisdom lies in rolling on, though,
Heartaches drive you back to the days gone.

Life is but a cul-de sac, where,
People stab you instantly at your back.
These modern-day Brutus with Satan's smile,
Don't hesitate to accompany you that extra
mile.

They exchange sweet nothings, show concern,
In fact, they are dying of heart burn.
Let good sense prevail on those senseless souls,
Who have taken the role of ghouls.

The Bitter Reality

Unsaid differences crop up,
When things don't go the way,
you want them to be.
Life just becomes like rime,
Waiting to lose its existence....

And it does, once it gets sunshine,
It goes on melting....
And melting till nothing is left!

Wonder how it loses its existence!
Its identity as well is lost amidst,
The snowy peaks and lofty mountains.

Snow, which seems to be so calm,
So serene, so pure and so dazzling fresh!
Is no more when the
Sun shines high in the sky.

Alas! Grim state of affairs results
In many a people losing their sheen,
And succumbing to pressures of life,
And we lose countless precious lives.

(This picture of Pelling Skywalk to Chenrezig Statue near Sanga Choeling, in Sikkim, clicked by me is one of my favourites. I visited the place in January 2020. It was a chilly morning and climbing up as if into the clouds, was just next to impossible for me, but the faith kept me going.)

Can We Hope for a Miracle?

Life, like a wheel, is forced to run,

It suffers great losses throughout,

Till it kicks the bucket,

When no one seems to be yours,

Except Shinigami!

That darkness is there again,

Those chilly winds are there again,

What will happen to life?

When one is not able to bear any more?

Why is everything so gloomy?

Why is everyone concerned about only the self?

God why did you create mankind?

When everyone has to suffer like this, solitary?

Is there any light at the end of the tunnel?

Will there be any light at the end of the tunnel?

Or it's just going to be yet another blind alley?

Forming New Bonds

Waiting for just a glimpse of yours,

In that part of the world,

Was as exciting, as joyous, as

Waiting for a glimpse of my close ones,

In this part of the world.

Life is nothing without you or

Without them !

I wonder why old bonds are side lined,

to create new ones?

(I remember writing this poem when I was pursuing graduation. A close friend's sister, pregnant, was abandoned by her husband a few months after their marriage. I didn't know and still don't know the reason. I was terribly moved by the incident and it just resulted in this short poem.)

Lonely Life

Oh God! What a lonely life is she leading!
Her life is as dark as a night,
For her there is no hope of light.

God help her, please help her settle,
What happened to her life partner?
They should have faith between them.
Otherwise, why ever did they wed?

What will the child do after infancy?
Who will he ask about his father?
Isn't it fair that at least for the infant?
They should reunite,
And lead a happy, joyful life?

In this cruel game of elders,

It is the innocent unborn who suffer,

What is his sin oh God!

Tell me or I will doubt your existence,

Not for once but for ever.

When the Days Are Gloomy

Death! O spouse of life!
Your silence appeals me!
Conquer my heart!
Conquer my body!
Conquer my soul!

Take me away with you,
When I am asleep,
Dreaming of things which aren't going to be true,
Tread softly, slowly and take me away,
To your own big world.

You are the conqueress!
You are the empress!
Of our whole being.
You give us peace, the eternal peace!

Which is not possible in this world,

Which is mad in the rat race for money.

One thinks of you in pain and suffering,

'Cos you are the one who will,

Help us in getting rid of your spouse- Life!

How strange! You both try to conquer us to your sides,

But you follow each other,

Life follows death and death follows life.

Oh Village!

Far away from the maddening noise,

I went to thee; you attracted me.

In the hours of weariness,

When my soul was frustrated,

I needed you most and you consoled me.

Early morning, I saw you happy!

The hymns being chanted, perhaps,

 In a nearby temple made me purer,

The jingling of that soft music,

Had the desired effect on me.

Village, O village, in your simplicity,

You appeal to people,

And give them that tranquillity,

Which is needed by them.

I woke up and walked down on an untrodden
path,

There it seemed, nature had hidden away,

All its beauty, the cool breeze slapped me,

The crops hummed and buzzed,

The dragonfly danced,

The early bird, in search of a worm,

The farmers busy with their crop,

The ladies taking the warm, fresh milk home,

The children crying, as it was early morning and

they had to accompany their parents.

It looked so fine; everyone was busy,

And still there was peace,

which is no longer found here.

I remembered you on the way,

I didn't want to go back, but I had to,

So, adieu my friend,

Again, in the moments of frustrations,

I will certainly come back to you.

To My Friend with Love

Today, oh only today I needed you the most!
To tell you that I need you, that I love you!
My friend! life is so miserable without you.

Those were the days when,
You and I would sit together,
Read and then chat together for a long time.

I would always win and tell you,
Dear! Don't depend on others,
Be independent,
Listen only to your conscience and no one else.

You always turned a deaf ear to my advice,
And that's the cause of your suffering.

You are suffering because you were,

Wholly and solely dependent on him,

He who shattered your dreams and ruined you.

Now again I repeat,

Dear! Don't depend on others,

Be independent.

Write your own destiny,

And see the change in you.

STop wars
IMAGINE
PEACE

High Hopes

And today, the fathers of this world say,
We should work for humanity and bring,
Brotherhood, equality and fraternity.

Yes! They will bring it for sure!
With people dying away in Ethiopia,
Not getting a morsel to eat,
To kill their hunger.

The children with skeletons,
And bulging eyes, show a mark of hope,
And the hope will come true,
When humanity will be demolished!

Prized Possessions

Emerging from the two eyes, slowly trickling down,

You are the precious pearls!

Lakhs of people keep you stored,

And wait subconsciously for a moment, to shed you away.

Tears, you are great!

You are a partner in both- the joys and the woes!

Tears! You are impartial!

You are hidden deep down in the bosom,

Your outburst makes others,

Drown uncontrollably….

Tears, you are the jewels of eyes!

In holding you close, the heart chokes,

In shedding you, the heart breaks the dams,

Tears you come to the fore,

And celebrate joys and sorrows alike!

My Heart – A Desert

The desert of my heart,
Breaks in a sigh or two.
It loves the loneliness,
And is happy,
When the faded moments,
Come alive like life.

Oh! They are so freshening, so soothing!
I don't wait for happiness,
I'd go to a dark place in future,
And build a castle of all sweet and sour
memories,
And be happy there.

The castle would be all in all for me,
For it'll be carrying the remembrances of
friends,
Once so close, so dear to me.

The idea of losing them,

Transports me to a grave...

Oh grave! unfold yourself,

And accept me, for then I would not be alone

but

You and me sharing my memoirs,

And listening to each other,

Slowly, and understanding each other.......

If only the world was not so happy!

If only it wore that deserted look!

Which my heart carries now and

will perhaps carry forever......

The Elusive Sleep

(I wrote this poem after I lost a very dear friend to an ailment. I was shattered beyond words; she was a very important part of my life. I carry her fond memories in my heart till date. It is so difficult to wipe out those memories which we had created over the years. Stay happy my dear wherever you are.)

Sleep! I am calling you,

Why don't you come to me?

Your drifting away makes me more aware of the world,

Of the miseries and my friends whom I have lost,

You always leave me alone at those intense moments,

when I need you the most,

Like you did just now......

I am awake, totally awake,

And thinking of future which is so difficult to

perceive,

So full of uncertainties!!

Sleep come to me and help me,

in getting rid of these dreary thoughts,

That keep coming to me time and again,

Although my life without them,

Would be more deserted, more solitary……

But no! Now I wish you go away, so far away,

That I never see you again,

So that I can write about what

I feel when I am so desperate,

I want to perish in peace while,

Thinking about my loved ones,

The beautiful souls who have departed,

They were precious gifts from God.

Come to me once and only once,

When I'll be tired of writing and

eagerly waiting for you.

When I am tired and totally tired of the

world.…...

Come slowly and embrace me,

And never leave me again.

Sufferings and Loneliness

Sadness and misery surround the man,
He is not sure of himself, he deceives himself,
By having desires and hopes that,
Some good will come at last.

The life passes away, becomes pale in searching
for a place which has some peace,
Some good stored for him,
But all is vain.......

Please, oh! please, don't be optimistic,
Accept what life has bestowed you with,
Don't look for future as,
What has to come will come,
Why to make life loathsome, burdensome and
troublesome?

In hoping for the best and that too when,

It is not going to come to you.

Look at him! Leaning at the table,

He has spent hours finding solutions,

To mysteries, but in vain!

He is sure of success,

SUCCESS that is proud and deludes him.

Don't deceive yourself.

Life is a mystery and one leaves the world,

Trying to solve the mystery of the unknown,

But life has remained what it was centuries ago!

It is hungry and wants you.

Envy, jealousy, selfish motives,

Are its progenies and they engulf you.

Don't try to make life smooth as

What has to come will come.

Don't, please don't be optimistic,

Accept what life has given you,

Come out of that vicious girdle,

Girdle that life has engulfed you with.

You and Me

I don't remember how oft

I wake up in the hush of the night,

And go to the balcony, sit there,

And remember those old days.

Movement of the leaves makes me,

Feel like you are coming,

The cool breeze makes me drink the chalice,

And forget the miseries of the world.

I remember you and feel only your presence
around,

The twilight is here and I come back,

to my senses and I think how happy,

I was in those hours when,

You and only me,

Would be with each other.

Parting from Friends

And today, after a long time
I'll leave.
Heart is bursting and wants to convey
something,
Eyes seem to understand the sentiment
but fail to reflect it,
Perhaps they think it is better,
To keep quiet on such occasions.

They have confidence that,
they will meet in near future.
So, adieu my friends, adieu to you all!
Till we meet again.

In Pursuit of Happiness

Life teaches us lessons, not easy to comprehend.

But why do the experiences have to be bitter?

Can't the riddles of life be understood sans rage?

Why can't we all be together in this learning experience?

Where we treat each other as travellers to a common dwelling!

Where each of us is on a pilgrimage, till we reach our destination.

Let us fill everyone's life with love.

Let us be polite and understanding.

Let us make each other's path smooth.

Let us remove the thorns of obstruction.

And be HUMANS in the true sense!

Let us make life worth living,

For people, for flora and for fauna.

Thinking Aloud

Our egos are huge, our hearts are small,

We expect people around us to be at our beck
and call,

And we refuse to budge.

Since time immemorial, we humans have been
like this.

We always want things to be our way

We are not ready to compromise,

We snap the bonds, if the others

around us don't think likewise.

We cause ceaseless suffering and pain to others,

And not once do we regret our decisions.

(I wrote this poem on my 20th birthday - many years back but I am using the picture of a cake baked recently by my daughter. What could be a better picture than this one! It's her creativity blended with mine!)

To Me on My Twentieth Birthday!

Twenty years have passed,

And it seems as if I was born yesterday!

All is so new, everything is so good,

I've seen life, lived life and observed life,

I witnessed coming and going of so many,

It always made me cry,

To see someone going away from me.

I can't forget those, who left me,

They were so dear, so close to me.

The idea of leaving them once,

Had broken my heart, but,

It had to come and it came,

To take them away.

Flowers still bloom, rains still fall, rainbows still form,

Everything around seems to have,

A sign of their touch, their presence.

Twenty years! you have given me so much,

That I want to thank you,

For all these experiences you gave me,

You told me who is true and who is false to me,

I owe you a lot.

Woes of Humanity

The night was young and yet the silence was killing,

The air was still but their looks were killing,

The hearts were crying and the owls were shrieking,

The eyes were open but the head was reeling!

I saw all at the altars kneeling,

Thinking of the past and the gone, praying,

Hearts broken and eyes overflowing,

People overwhelmed and thoughts reverberating!

Prayer meetings were held at the church and the temples,

Prayer meetings were held at the mosques and the synagogues,

Each family unit lamenting its loss!!!

And up there the God in the heaven,

Smiling at the pettiness of humans,

For they don't the rules of the humanity abide,

And remain happy if religions divide!!

A Student Reminisces....

(I wrote this poem when my son was in grade XI and his class was bidding farewell to their seniors. My son too would leave the school the next year and I just scribbled these words thinking of him and his friends who were quite close to me also.)

Only yesterday was I a child,
Holding the finger of my mother,
She'd lead me to the classroom,
Where my teacher, with a smile on her face,
Would try to enliven my mood and brighten my face.

With tears in my eyes, I'd leave my home,
Howling and crying, trying to adjust in the school.
Selfless love of my teachers and company of my friends,

Somehow pulled me through and I overcame
the blues.

How this journey of twelve years got over?
I just do not know.
It's over before I even realized.
Today at this junction, when I am about to
leave the school,
To face the harsh selfish world outside,

I again feel like a kid,
Now, not wanting to leave,
My second home- school.

The feelings are again the same,
There's a lump in my heart,
Tears in my eyes, although I don't show them.

When I, now am leaving the school,
I want the same tender care and selfless love

of yours (my teachers),
Who have given their best to me.

Well, I agree, the journey might have been
turbulent,
There might have been countless arguments,
scolding and beatings,
We might have been very mischievous at times!
But then, isn't it a part of growing up?
Won't you excuse us as we were mindless,
immature kids?

Today, when I sit with you one last time like
this,
My eyes swell with tears and my heart is
choked.
Forgive me if I have been rude, impatient and
bad.
I need your blessing before I face the world,
The thought that these safe walls will not be
there,

is painful and makes me shudder,

But I know when I close my eyes, you will be there.

Just as my elders, pray for me that I'm successful,

While every breath of mine remains indebted to you.

(My daughter knows my longing for Kashmir, the forgotten land of my forefathers. I got really sentimental when two years back, she procured these daffodils for me and kept them on the table before I reached back home from work. The fragrance drifted me to the valley. Sad, but this is how I have kept Kashmir alive in my heart)

Going Down the Memory Lane

Memories, memories and memories!
This is what I brought from my land.
The bonding is so strong that
I realize it was never gone.

It was like embers simmering from within,
Until this recent visit flared it up.
With misty eyes, I left the valley,
Not knowing when to return.

It is just difficult, just impossible to stop the time,
And go back to those years, so precious!
So much water has flown down the Jhelum......
Those dams can't be built which can stop,
The eyes and the hearts from overflowing.

This land of my forefathers, this land of mine,

Will always remain close to my heart,

Falling leaves return to their roots, they say,

My heart just aches to return to my strife torn
valley.

.... .. Do dreams ever come true?

Far from My Roots

The glorious past that was once ours,

Is not ours anymore!

We long for it, we cry for it, we plead for it,

But alas! Who is there?

The memories are still so fresh, so new…

It seems it was just yesterday,

When I would enjoy my trips to the valley,

When I would go around the Dal Lake, cycling.

Where each stone, each brick, each wall and
each brook,

Had a story of our ancestors to tell…

I have not visited Ksheer Bhawani, our sacred
temple!

I have not visited Khrew, the temple of Fire, my
family deity!

I ramble like a wanderer in search of my lost
identity!

Is there any power on Earth that can restore all
that is lost to me, to us?

We all are scattered like a broken string of
pearls,

In search of our identity, in search of those
whom we have lost,

In this barbaric act of a few,

We are just reduced to a handful.

The wounds are still green, not yet healed,

My heart returns to my land which is no longer
mine,

I shudder to think of the losses of life we had
to suffer.

My heart still laments the loss of those,

Who could not even feel the soil of their land of
birth!

Who could not breathe their last in their own land!

Who were deprived of their right to go back to their sacred place!

Even my life will fade away without a glimpse of my land

Is there anyone as unlucky as us – the Kashmiri Pandits?

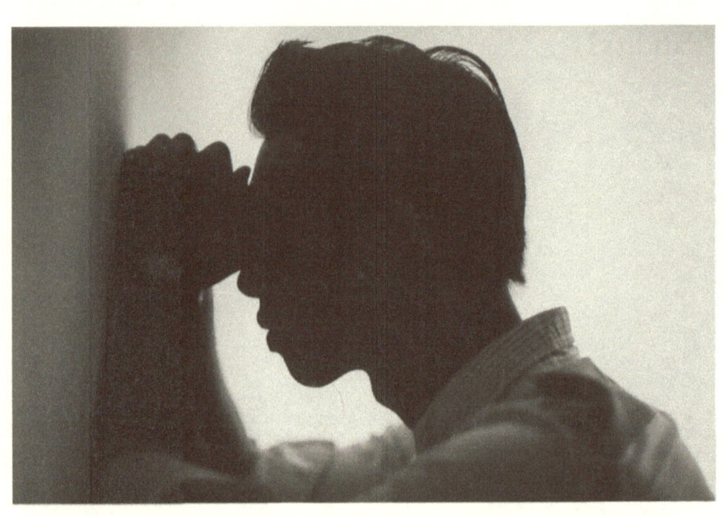

दर्द भरा दिल

इस दर्द भरे दिल से अब तो,

आहें ही निकल सकती है,

वो दिन गए जब विश्वास की

एक लहर थी हमारे-तुम्हारे बीच,

जब विश्वास ही न था मुझ पर,

तो क्यों कर चले थे प्यार जताने?

अब तो जीवन मेरा सिर्फ एक धारा है,

न जाने कहाँ, कब, कोई सहारा मिले ।

मौत रुपी विशाल समुद्र में जाने से पहले,

मैं सिर्फ यही चाहती हूँ कि मुझे कोई और किनारा मिले,

व मैं ज़िन्दगी भर यह सोचती रहूँ,

कि यह क्या हुआ, क्यों हुआ, कैसे हुआ?

लहर

जल में उठ रही थी लहरें,

लहरों को जल में भी यूं, तड़पता देख

लगा मुझे ऐसे कि,

जैसे इनकी कोई अधूरी रही है चाह ,

तभी तो पवन के इस स्पर्श से,

ये, न जाने क्यों भर्ती है आह!

इस आह व इस तड़पन से,

मुझे भी कुछ अजीब सा लगता है,

न जाने क्यों लहरों को देख,

मेरे दिल में भय उत्पन्न होता है,

जिस तरह से मैं विश्व से अलग हो,

अपना एक अलग अस्तित्व चाहती हूँ,

उसी तरह शायद ये लहर जल से अलग होना चाहती है,

पर क्योंकि यह असंभव है,

इसलिए जल में है तरंग,

व मुझमें जीने की है उमंग।

Dowry
system

शहनाई

शहनाइयों की आवाज़ से न जाने क्यों,

मुझ पर उदासी सी छा जाती है,

अजीब सी हलचल एक, दिमाग पर छा जाती है,

मैं खुद यह सोचकर हूँ परेशान कि,

यह सब क्यों होता जा रहा है मुझे,

कैसे अजीब सा असर हो रहा है मुझ पर !

सोचकर अचानक याद आया कि ,

कहने को तो विवाह दो दिलों का मेल है ,

पर जो गत यह समाज इस बहु की बनाता है,

उसे देखकर दिल बस टूट कर रह जाता है ।

काश ,कि दूसरे की बेटी को होता समझा अपना !

तो विवश बाप को न यह दिन पड़ता देखना,

कहने को बहू जला तो दी जाती है पर,

क्या माँ बाप के हृदय से उसकी याद निकल पाती है?

आँसू बहाते, उस बेटी की याद में यूँ ही,

उम्र उनकी गुज़र जाती है ।

दहेज नाम की यह बीमारी कितनों को,

अपने में समेट कर ले जाती है।

MEMORIES

खट्टी मीठी यादें

रिश्तों की नाज़ुकता का अहसास,
अब कितना नाज़ुक / नया सा है?
न चाहते हुए भी यह ज़िन्दगी,
कितना कुछ दिखा सा रही है।

ये रिश्ते, यह बंधन कितने प्यारे से है?
यहीं यह ज़िन्दगी एहसास करा सा रहीं है।
न तोड़ों, न झकझोरो, इन अटूट धागों को,
जो टूटे, न जुड़ पाएंगे कभी।

जो इक बार छूट गए पीछे,
वे न मिल पाएंगे कभी,
तन्हाइयों में आ कर क्या
न सताएँगे हमें?

सभी यादें, कुछ खट्टी, कुछ मीठी, कुछ कड़वी,
इस दिल में संजोए बढ़े चलो।

ज़िंदगी

ज़िंदगी से मिलने से पहले

सोचा था कि ज़िंदगी मधुर है,

नव-नव स्वपन लिए जब मैं,

मग्न रहती थी प्रकृति के कण-कण में,

तब कभी न सोचा था कि

एक यह दिन भी आएगा,

धूल बन कर के ज़िंदगी व

मेरे मधुर स्वपन ले जाएगा ।

आज भी जब सोचती हूँ उस क्षण के लिए,

कसक सी उठती है हृदय में,

सब कुछ खो जाता है इधर-उधर,

रह जाता है अंधेरा, बस अंधेरा और मैं,

क्या यही है वह ज़िंदगी,

जिस पर मानव इठलाता है ?

एक मधुर याद को लेकर स्वपनों में खो जाता है।

जीवन

यह जीवन है क्या?

एक स्वपन ही तो है यह और वह भी अधूरा,

नितदिन नए नए स्वपन लिए जब,

यह मानव नया उठता है,

हर स्वपन को साकार करने की,

कोशिश में रहता है, मगर कोई यह बताए

कि यह जीवन है क्या?

एक स्वपन ही तो है यह और वह भी अधूरा,

सोते समय व हर पल मैं बस यही सोचती हूँ,

कि जब तक आकाश है, यह पृथ्वी है,

यह सागर है, या जब तक यह संसार है,

यह जीवन तो वही रहेगा, सदा अधूरा, अधूरा, अधूरा,

यही सोच कि अगले जन्म में होगा यह पूरा,

सो जा मानव, कल अभी आना है नया सवेरा,

शायद आशा की नव किरण लिए आए यह सवेरा !

तन्हाई

रात्रि के इस गहन अंधकार में

दीपक की लौ देख कर जगमग,

आशा की किरण एक दी दिखाई!

शायद वही मंजिल हो मेरी, शायद हो यही तकदीर मेरी,

उस प्रीतम की शायद यही हो आवाज़,

कि मैं देख संकू उसे हर पल हर रात ।

निकट होते हुए भी मुझे इस दूरी का है आभास,

इन बंधनों को तोड़ कर तू,

तन्हाइयों में याद कर के मुझे,

इस दूरी का फिर हुआ अहसास मुझे,

इस संसार में होते हुए भी कितने लाचार हैं हम,

साथ-साथ होते हुए भी कितने दूर हैं हम,

यही तो खेल है इस सृष्टि का,

दूर करने के बाद कभी देती है निकटता।

प्रकृति

गगन के उस छोर की ओर देख,

पेड़ो व हवाओं के इस मिलन को देख,

न जाने लगा क्यों मुझे कुछ ऐसा,

कि जैसे प्रकृति है सिर्फ एक धोखा,

तभी तो पेड़ व हवा के मिलन के बाद,

भड़कती हुई आँधियों के बाद,

रह जाता है पेड़ कहीं व आँधी कहीं,

कितनी सदियों के इंतज़ार के बाद मगर,

जब वृक्ष को मिलती है पवन की समीपता,

तो वह बह जाता है उस लय में,

व प्रकृति का नियम चलता है दोबारा।

ऐसा ही होता आया है सदियों से,

ऐसे ही रहेगा हमेशा यह चक्र सदा।

सूना आँचल

(I remember jotting down these words when a colleague of mine lost his grown-up son. I shudder even now when I think of that day. Dreams were shattered and life lost its meaning for me. Some pains just stay forever……)

समय कुछ थम सा गया है,

हर आँसू कहीं खो सा गया है,

जी कर भी क्या करें हम?

हर जिया हुआ पल जो,

कहीं खो सा गया है।

क्या करें उन यादों का?

जो तुम्हीं तक तो सीमित थीं,

क्या करें उन ख़्वाबों का?

जो तुम्हें लेकर ही तो संजोए थे।

तुम्हें खो के क्या खोया है मैंने ?

मेरा सूना आँचल ही जानता है,

जो हर बदली हुई करवट को खोजता है ।

9 798886 066883